The ULTIMATE CHALLENGE BOOK

Buster Books

WRITTEN AND EDITED BY GARY PANTON
ILLUSTRATED BY HARRY BRIGGS
COVER DESIGNED BY JOHN BIGWOOD

The publisher and authors disclaim as far as legally permissible all liability for accidents or injuries or loss that may occur as a result of information or instructions in this book.

First published in Great Britain in 2021 by Buster Books,
an imprint of Michael O'Mara Books Limited,
9 Lion Yard, Tremadoc Road, London SW4 7NQ

 www.mombooks.com/buster
Buster Books
@BusterBooks

Copyright © Buster Books 2021

A CIP catalogue record for this book is available from the British Library.

ISBN: 978-1-78055-719-9

2 4 6 8 10 9 7 5 3 1

Papers used by Buster Books are natural, recyclable products made of wood from well-managed, FSC®-certified forests and other controlled sources. The manufacturing processes conform to the environmental regulations of the country of origin.

This book was printed in December 2020 by Leo Paper Products Ltd, Heshan Astros Printing Ltd, Xuantan Temple Industrial Zone, Gulao Town, Heshan City, Guangdong Province, China.

CONTENTS

HOW THIS BOOK WORKS

This book is full of games, challenges and tasks that you can try out to **test yourself** and **best yourself.**

Some of the challenges can be done indoors. With others, take your book outdoors for more space. Most can be done completely on your own, while with others you can compete against friends or family. The important thing is having fun!

For some of the challenges, you'll need some equipment — but if you don't have it, it doesn't matter. You can either use something else, or move on to another challenge that involves different stuff.

Remember: practice makes perfect, which is why a lot of the challenges have space for you to write down your scores from a few separate attempts. Once you've done that, it's easy to work out which score is your life's greatest work. Plus, there's more space at the back of the book for making extra notes and fiendish plans.

Are you ready? It's time to find out ...
what's **YOUR** Personal Best?

THE RULES

1. Don't do any of the challenges at school. If you do, it'll make your teachers go all grumpy.
2. If you have to use anything that isn't yours, ask permission first.
3. Don't break anything.
4. Don't waste food.
5. No cheating.
6. When you're done, put things back where you got them.

ONE-PLAYER CHALLENGES

These games all need one thing: you!
(But don't worry — some of them include
ideas involving a friend, too.)

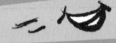

TRY NOT TO LAUGH

Load up the funniest videos you can think of. Tried and tested howlers that never fail to make you **GUFFAW**. The sort of videos that make milk come shooting out of your nose (even when you haven't been drinking any milk).

Watch one after the other and time yourself trying your hardest not to laugh. How long can you last?

Attempt 1: .... seconds

Attempt 2: .... seconds

Attempt 3: .... seconds

Make a note of the the funniest videos here, and put a massive tick next to the one that made you laugh the most.

.... ☐

.... ☐

.... ☐

.... ☐

.... ☐

TAKE A STAND

Can you stand up for exactly two minutes? Here's how it works:

1. While sitting down, press 'start' on a timer.

2. Now stand up, **QUICK!**

3. When you think **exactly two minutes** have passed, stop your timer. No peeking!

4. Sit down and check your time.

HOW DID YOU DO?

Attempt 1: .... seconds

Attempt 2: .... seconds

Attempt 3: .... seconds

SNEAKY HINT

Count up the seconds in your head. You need 120 seconds, and each second takes roughly the amount of time that it would take you to say 'one armadillo'.

OTHER THINGS YOU CAN TRY DOING FOR EXACTLY TWO MINUTES

PLANKING (THAT'S LYING ON YOUR FRONT WITH YOUR ARMS BY YOUR SIDES)

HOPPING UP AND DOWN

DANCING

BALANCING ONE SHOE ON YOUR HEAD

PATTING YOUR HEAD WHILE RUBBING YOUR TUMMY

PICK UP A PEA

Anyone can pick up peas,
right? Well, how about doing it ...
WITH CHOPSTICKS? DUN DUN DUNNNN!

Get yourself a bowl of frozen peas, put an empty
bowl next to it and see how many peas you can move
from one bowl to the other with your chopsticks.

You have one minute. Your time starts ...

NOW!

WRITE YOUR PEA TOTALS HERE

Attempt 1: .... peas

Attempt 2: .... peas

Attempt 3: .... peas

NO PEAS? NO PROBLEM! TRY USING THESE INSTEAD ...

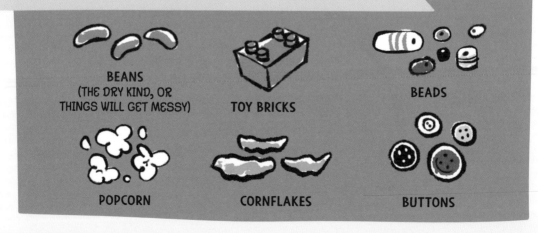

BEANS
(THE DRY KIND, OR
THINGS WILL GET MESSY)

TOY BRICKS

BEADS

POPCORN

CORNFLAKES

BUTTONS

COIN SNATCH

Put your hand on your shoulder and balance a coin on your elbow. Quick as a flash, swing your arm forwards and catch the coin before it drops.

THE WORLD RECORD COIN SNATCH WAS A PILE OF 328 COINS IN ONE GO!

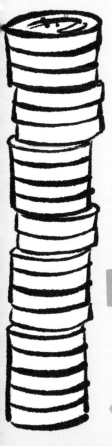

How many tries did you need before you caught it?

....

How many times in a row can you catch the coin without dropping it?

WRITE YOUR RECORD HERE

....

LET'S MAKE THIS HARDER

Snatching one coin is too easy! It's time to do it with a whole stack of 'em! What's the biggest stack of coins you can catch?

COLOUR IN HOW MANY YOU MANAGED

FLIPPING AWESOME

It's time to **FLIP IT GOOD**. Take a plastic bottle, fill it halfway with water and throw it up into the air so that it rotates before landing perfectly on its bottom. Ta-da!

Try it 20 times. How many times did it land perfectly? ....

Have you become a **FLIPPING MASTER**? Let's make this interesting. How many times in a flipping row can you do it?

Attempt 1: .... flips

Attempt 2: .... flips

Attempt 3: .... flips

CRUMB HEAD

Balance a cookie* on your forehead. You look great! You should do this more often. It's really working for you.

 Now for the tricky bit. Start a timer and see how quickly you can get the cookie from your forehead to your mouth without using your hands. Go!

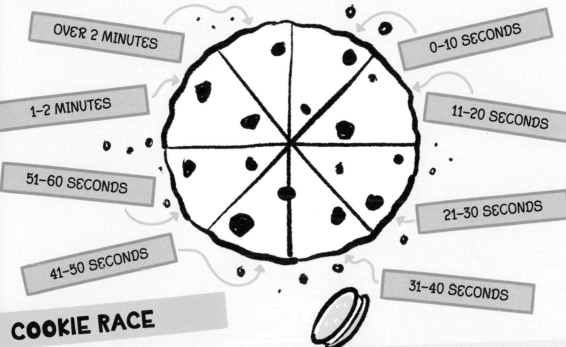

OVER 2 MINUTES

0–10 SECONDS

1–2 MINUTES

11–20 SECONDS

51–60 SECONDS

21–30 SECONDS

41–50 SECONDS

31–40 SECONDS

COOKIE RACE

With a friend, see which of you can send that cookie mouthwards the fastest. Make it best of three (or more if you're hungry).

Race 1 winner: ....

Race 2 winner: ....

Race 3 winner: ....

.... is the champion cookie racer.

*You could swap cookies for crackers if you want to try to be a bit healthier.

TAKE FLIGHT

How far can a paper plane fly?
Make the greatest plane in the history
of air travel (you can use the instructions
on the opposite page to help, if you like)
and record its papery adventures here.

Flight 1: ....

....

You don't need to use
a measuring tape if you
don't have one. You could
just write down where the
plane got to (e.g. 'Flight 1
made it to the end of the
sofa' or 'Flight 2 got lodged
in Grandma's hair').

Flight 2: ....

....

All the best aeroplanes have a fancy name, like The White Flyer,
Sheets of Fury or Old Mrs Wings. Give your plane a name here:

....

WITH A FRIEND

WOWEE!

THE FURTHEST EVER
PAPER PLANE FLIGHT
TRAVELLED JUST
UNDER 70 METRES.

Start a timer, give yourselves five
minutes and see who can come up with
the best paper plane. Test your designs
out by seeing whose plane flies the
furthest. Good luck, young pilot!

....

made the best paper plane.

HOW TO MAKE A PAPER AEROPLANE

There are loads of ways to make a paper aeroplane.
Here's one of the most popular ways, to get you started.

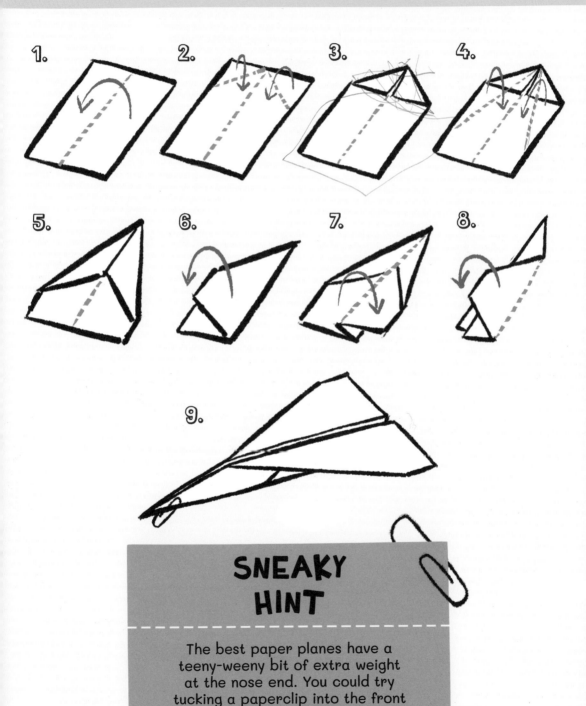

1.

2.

3.

4.

5.

6.

7.

8.

9.

SNEAKY HINT

The best paper planes have a
teeny-weeny bit of extra weight
at the nose end. You could try
tucking a paperclip into the front
of yours to see if it helps.

APPLE ASSASSIN

How quickly can you break an apple in half, using just your hands? Feel that snivelling apple shiver to its very core as you rip it in half and teach it a thing or two. It'll be the last apple that ever messes with you.

I ripped apart a pathetic, good-for-nothing apple in .... seconds.

FEEL MY FRUITY WRATH.

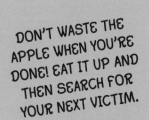

DON'T WASTE THE APPLE WHEN YOU'RE DONE! EAT IT UP AND THEN SEARCH FOR YOUR NEXT VICTIM.

DRAW A TERRIFIED FACE ON THIS APPLE

BAG SHOT

How far can you throw an empty shopping bag? The bag might be empty, but your sense of pride sure won't be!

Attempt 1: ....

Attempt 2: ....

Attempt 3: ....

If you don't have a measuring tape, just put some markers on the ground in front of you and see which one you can reach.

WITH A FRIEND

It's a question as old as time itself: who can throw their bag the furthest? There's only one way to find out ... have a bag-off!

WINNER'S NAME HERE

....

RUNNER UP'S NAME HERE

....

NOW TRY THROWING ...

A LEAF

A FEATHER

A BALLOON

A TISSUE
(AN UNUSED TISSUE, NOT A SNOTTY ONE, THANKS)

KEEPY UPPIES

Kick-ups? Keep-ups? Keepy uppies?
It's not what you call them that counts,
it's the mad skills you use when you do them.

How many times can you bounce a football off
your own body bits without it touching the ground?
You can use your feet, knees, thighs and shoulders,
but never your hands or it'll be a **RED CARD** for you!

Attempt 1: .... bounces

Attempt 2: .... bounces

Attempt 3: .... bounces

TOP TIP

If you're struggling, try letting
the ball bounce on the ground
once in-between kicks for the
first few practice efforts.

WITH A FRIEND

How many times can you keepy
uppy the ball back and forth
without it touching the ground?

WRITE YOUR
PERSONAL
BEST HERE

....

TOUGHER TRICKS

- Make it even harder by only using your left foot if you're right-handed, or your right foot if you're left-handed.

- Getting really good? Try bouncing the ball once on your right foot, then your right knee, then your right thigh ... then doing the same again on your left side, all without it touching the ground.

- How many keepy uppies can you do ... WITH YOUR EYES CLOSED?

TIME TRIAL

How many keepy uppies can you do in a minute?
Fill in this handy pie chart to record your best attempt.

OVER 40!

31–40

26–30

21–25

0–5

6–10

11–15

16–20

NOW TRY DOING KEEPY UPPIES WITH ...

A TINY BALL
(LIKE A TENNIS BALL)

A MASSIVE BALL
(LIKE A BEACH BALL)

A BALLOON

A STUFFED TOY

MILK BOWLING

Ladies. Gentlemen. **LET'S BOWL.** All you need to make your own bowling alley is some flat ground, a little ball and some empty milk or juice cartons.

How many cartons can you knock over with each roll?

Attempt 1: .... cartons

Attempt 2: .... cartons

Attempt 3: .... cartons

TOP TIP

Make yourself feel like a real bowling pro by doing this challenge in mismatching shoes.

EXTREME MILK BOWLING

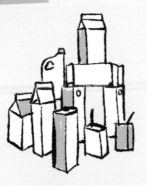

ROLL YOUR BALL FROM FURTHER AWAY

ADD LOADS OF EXTRA CARTONS

FILL THE CARTONS WITH WATER TO MAKE THEM HEAVIER

ROLL THE BALL BACKWARDS

CUP PYRAMID

Recreate the majestic wonders of ancient Egypt, using paper cups.

How many cups can you stack into your pyramid, without it falling down?

....

SNEAKY HINT

TWENTY-ONE IS A GOOD NUMBER OF CUPS FOR THIS CHALLENGE. YOU CAN STACK YOUR CUPS LIKE THIS.

TIME TRIAL

Now that you're a pyramid pro, see how many times you can build your pyramid and take it apart again, in two minutes.

Attempt 1: .... times

Attempt 2: .... times

Attempt 3: .... times

RAP CHAMP

So you want to be a **BIG-TIME RAPPER**? See how long you can last if you're only allowed to speak in rhyme. (This is how all the best rappers started out, honest.)

How many rhymes were in your best raps?

Rap 1: .... rhymes

Rap 2: .... rhymes

Rap 3: .... rhymes

Keep a note of your favourite raps here (there's also some extra space at the back of the book).

....

....

....

....

WHAT'S YOUR RAPPER NAME?*

....

*Your rapper name is your first initial, followed by the name of the last thing you ate. Excellent examples include J-Candy, P-Cornflake and G-Meatball.

HAVE A RAP-OFF

With a friend, take it in turns to come up with a rhyme for each other's lines, just like this ...

Spooky ghost

Cheese on toast

Burger and fries

Elephant's thighs

Sitting on a log

With a sausage dog

NOW WRITE IN YOUR OWN ONES

....

....

....

....

....

....

WHOEVER CAN KEEP GOING THE LONGEST IS THE RAP CHAMP!

TIPPY-TOE TRIAL

How long can you stay
on your tippy-toes for?
On your marks ... get set ... GO!

Attempt 1: .... seconds

Attempt 2: .... seconds

Attempt 3: .... seconds

EXTREME TIPPY-TOES

Not tough enough for you? Try attempting some of these
fiendish feats at the same time.

**BALANCE ON
ONE LEG**

**JUMP UP
AND DOWN**

**POUR YOURSELF A
NICE COLD DRINK
OF WATER**

**PRETEND TO BE A
HAPPY LITTLE HORSE**

CARD CASTLE

All you need for this is a pack of cards, a flat surface and a **very** steady hand. Balance your cards on their ends so they lean against each other, just like in this very helpful picture.

How many cards can you get into your tower without it collapsing?

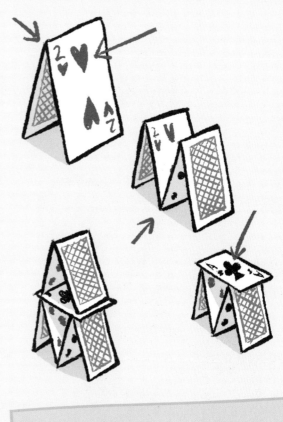

DRAW YOUR CARD CASTLE HERE, WITH YOU STANDING PROUDLY IN FRONT OF IT AS ITS KING OR QUEEN.

Attempt 1: .... cards

Attempt 2: .... cards

Attempt 3: .... cards

Give your Card Castle a name, like Fortress of Me, Ace Towers or The Palace of Awesome.

COPY CAT

This is Snuggles the cat. Aw, just look at the little guy.
Actually, take a good look, because now you have
to draw him on the opposite page ...
BLINDFOLDED*!

*The blindfold should go on you, not Snuggles.

DRAW
SNUGGLES
HERE

1. What even is that? ☐

2. We must never speak of this again. ☐

3. Could do better. ☐

4. Not bad, but why do his eyes look like that? ☐

5. It's like looking at an actual cat! ☐

CARD NINJA

For this one you will need:

- A pack of cards
- A bucket (or hat, or bowl)
- The skills of a mystical ninja

Stand as far away from the bucket as you can, and throw the cards one at a time. **How many can you get into the bucket?** You have one minute!

Attempt 1: .... cards

Attempt 2: .... cards

Attempt 3: .... cards

NIFTY NINJA BONUS ROUNDS

THROW TWO CARDS AT ONCE

THROW THE CARDS FROM YOUR TOES

THROW WITH YOUR BACK TURNED TO THE BUCKET

REPLACE THE BUCKET WITH AN ITTY-BITTY PLANT POT

CRACKERS!

How quickly can you eat three dry crackers? Your goal is to do it in under two minutes. Good luck, Cracker Comrade. And remember: drinking is cheating!

NO CRACKERS?
TRY USING DRY PIECES OF BREAD INSTEAD.

COLOUR IN THE CRACKER CHART WITH YOUR TIME TALLY

OVER 120 SECONDS

111–119 SECONDS

101–110 SECONDS

91–100 SECONDS

81–90 SECONDS

61–80 SECONDS

31–60 SECONDS

0–30 SECONDS

WITH A FRIEND

Make it a race! The fastest one to munch their lovely dry crackers wins.

TOO EASY?

After finishing your tasty, crumbly crackers, try whistling the national anthem — all the way to the end!

TONGUE TWISTERS

How quickly can you read out all of these
terrific tongue twisters without slipping up?
If you make a mistake, you have to start again!

Fuzzy wuzzy was a bear.
Fuzzy wuzzy had no hair.
Fuzzy wuzzy wasn't very
fuzzy, was he?

How much wood would
a woodchuck chuck,
If a woodchuck could
chuck wood?

Red lorry, yellow lorry,
Red lorry, yellow lorry,
Red lorry, yellow lorry,
Red lorry, yellow lorry.

I scream, you scream,
We all scream for ice cream.

She sells seashells on the seashore,
The shells she sells are seashells I'm sure,
So if she sells seashells on the seashore,
Then I'm sure she sells seashore shells.

Peter Piper picked a peck of pickled peppers.
Did Peter Piper pick a peck of pickled peppers?
If Peter Piper picked a peck of pickled peppers,
Where's the peck of pickled peppers Peter Piper picked?

Betty Botter bought a bit of butter.
The butter Betty Botter bought was a bit bitter
and made her batter bitter.
But a bit of better butter makes better batter.
So Betty Botter bought a bit of better butter,
making Betty Botter's bitter batter better.

If you must cross a coarse, cross cow
across a crowded cow crossing, cross
the cross, coarse cow across the
crowded cow crossing carefully.

It took me .... seconds to read the tongue

twisters out and I had to start again .... times.

**WRITE YOUR OWN TONGUE TWISTER HERE AND CHALLENGE A FRIEND
TO SAY IT PERFECTLY.**

....

....

....

....

....

SILENCE!

How long can you last without uttering a peep? That's NO TALKING. And also no whispering, yelling, coughing, sniffing, sneezing, gulping, burping or windy-pops of any nature.

WRITE YOUR TIMES HERE

Attempt 1: ....

Attempt 2: ....

Attempt 3: ....

NOW TRY STAYING SILENT WHILE ...

SOMEONE TICKLES YOU

EATING NACHOS (NO CRUNCHING!)

DRINKING A SPOONFUL OF LEMON JUICE

READING THE JOKES ON THE NEXT PAGE

How do you make a tissue dance?
Put a little boogie in it.

What do you call a cow on a trampoline?
A milk shake.

Why did the tomato blush?
Because it saw the salad dressing.

What did the nose say to the finger?
Stop picking on me.

Why did the tap-dancer quit?
She kept falling in the sink.

What's brown and sticky?
A stick.

What did one plate say to the other plate?
Dinner is on me.

How does the moon cut his hair?
Eclipse it.

How do you make an octopus laugh?
With ten-tickles!

What did one toilet say to the other toilet?
You look flushed.

THROW GOLF

This is just like actual golf, but instead of a club you have your arms, and instead of a hole you have a target, and instead of a golf ball you have literally any ball.

YOU'LL PROBABLY WANT TO DO THIS ONE OUTDOORS, SO YOU DON'T UPSET THE OLDS.

All you have to do is choose your target, decide how far from it you stand, and throw your ball at it. The fewer throws it takes to hit the target, the bigger a **THROW GOLF MASTER** you are.

Attempt 1: .... throws

Attempt 2: .... throws

Attempt 3: .... throws

THINGS **NOT** TO USE AS THROW GOLF TARGETS

| ANYTHING BREAKABLE | OTHER HUMANS (OR ANIMALS) | DOGGY POO BINS | DOGGY POO | BASICALLY, ANYTHING POO-RELATED |

LET'S HIT THE COURSE!

So you think you're pretty good at Throw Golf?
It's time to make your own Throw Golf course!

This is a great game to play at your local park. Decide how many targets you want to use, then work your way around your course, keeping count of your throws (you can use the score card below if you like). Trees, fence posts and goal posts all make great targets.

Either play on your own and become a **Top Secret Throw Golf Legend**, or make things extra-interesting and play against friends.

SCORE CARD

Your names			
Target 1			
Target 2			
Target 3			
Target 4			
Target 5			
Target 6			
Target 7			
Target 8			
Target 9			
FINAL SCORE			

REMEMBER: LOWEST SCORE WINS!

BRAIN FREEZE

For this one, you'll need:

- A timer
- An ice cube
- Your own head

Do you have those things? Strong start! Now all you need to do is balance the ice cube on top of your head, start the timer, and DO NOT REMOVE YOUR HANDS FROM YOUR SIDES UNDER **ANY** CIRCUMSTANCES.

IT'S TOUGHER (AND COLDER) THAN YOU THINK. HOW LONG CAN YOU LAST?

Attempt 1: .... seconds

Attempt 2: .... seconds

Attempt 3: .... seconds

Did you manage to keep your hands by your sides until the ice cube was completely gone? (N)ice work! Reward yourself by drying everything up with a towel and never speaking of this again.

OTHER THINGS TO TRY BALANCING ON YOUR HEAD

A TENNIS BALL

SEVERAL TEDDY BEARS

ONE SHOE

ALL OF THE PILLOWS FROM YOUR BED

LEANING TOWER OF COINS

Build the highest stack of coins known to humanity, without it toppling over.

DRAW YOUR ATTEMPTS HERE

Attempt 1   Attempt 2   Attempt 3

NOW TRY MAKING YOUR COIN TOWER ...

WHILE BLINDFOLDED

WHILE WEARING OVEN GLOVES

WITH YOUR FEET

WHILE BALANCING AN ICE CUBE ON YOUR HEAD

COIN SLIDE

Slide a coin across a table, towards the edge. Your mission is to get your coin to stop as close to the edge as possible, without it plummeting to the floor while shrieking "AAARRGGGHHH HELP ME I'M ONLY A TINY HELPLESS COIN, SOMEONE PLEASE HELP!"

DRAW A TINY CROWN ON TOP OF THIS COIN

Once you've slid a few coins, write down their finishing positions here*:

Coin 1: ....

Coin 2: ....

Coin 3: ....

Coin 4: ....

Coin 5: ....

VERY IMPORTANT ANNOUNCEMENT

BE SURE TO COVER THE TABLE WITH A CLOTH OR SOME SHEETS OF PAPER. NO ONE LIKES A SCRATCHED TABLE!

*If the coins end up too close to call, use a ruler to work out which one wins and stop the coins from all falling out with each other.

COIN COMBAT

It's time to put your new coin-sliding skills to the test against a friend. Take five coins each and take it in turns to slide 'em. If you feel like playing dirty, you can even try to nudge the other person's coin right off the edge towards certain doom. **BWAH-HA-HA!**

Whose coin won? ....

NO COINS? NO PROBLEM

You could use these instead ...

SWEETS   BUTTONS   TOY CARS   GRAPES

HARD CARDS

For this one, you need a pack of playing cards. Lay 10 cards down in front of you, facing upwards, and try to remember them. You get a minute to study them, before you have to turn them face-down. How many can you remember?

WITH EACH ATTEMPT, LAY DOWN 10 NEW CARDS.

Attempt 1: .... cards

Attempt 2: .... cards

Attempt 3: .... cards

HARDER CARDS

Easily remembering all 10 cards? You're way too good at this! Try using more cards, or giving yourself less time to study them, and it'll get harder!

EVEN HARDER CARDS

Lay 20 cards face-up, study them for a minute, then ask a friend to remove three of them while you look away. Your friend should rearrange the cards to hide where the gaps are. Can you say what the missing three cards are?

BOUNCY BOUNCY

How many times can you bounce a tennis ball on a racquet without dropping the ball? Use this page to record your best attempts forever, so that when historians find this book in a hundred years they'll think you were a famous tennis pro.

Attempt 1: .... bounces

Attempt 2: .... bounces

Attempt 3: .... bounces

WITH A FRIEND

See how many times you can hit a ball back and forth with racquets, without the ball touching the ground. It's like an actual game of tennis, but way better.

TRY REPLACING THE TENNIS BALL WITH ...

A BEACH BALL

A TEDDY BEAR YOU
DON'T CARE ABOUT
(ONE THAT LOOKS EVIL, FOR EXAMPLE)

A WET SPONGE

JUGGLE MASTER

These challenges work best with a little ball, such as a tennis ball. You should do them outdoors to avoid harming any poor, innocent light bulbs.

JUST ONE HAND

How many times in a row can you throw your ball up and catch it, using just one hand?

Attempt 1: .... catches

Attempt 2: .... catches

Attempt 3: .... catches

FASTER! FASTER!

Now, use a timer and see how many times you can catch your ball one-handed in a minute.

Attempt 1: .... catches

Attempt 2: .... catches

Attempt 3: .... catches

MORE BALLS, PLEASE

It's time for **actual juggling**. Get a second ball and time yourself. How long can you juggle two balls without dropping them?

Attempt 1: .... seconds

Attempt 2: .... seconds

Attempt 3: .... seconds

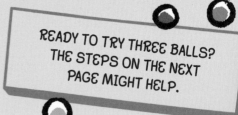

READY TO TRY THREE BALLS? THE STEPS ON THE NEXT PAGE MIGHT HELP.

1.

2.

3.

4.

5.

6.

TOP TIP

If it's too difficult with balls, beanbags are great for improving your juggling skills.

SPINNER WINNER

People think the best thing about coins is spending them on boring stuff like food and clothes, but they're wrong. The best thing about coins is SPINNING THEM.

How long can you spin a coin for? Record your best efforts here:

DID YOU KNOW?

ONE SPINNING MASTER IN JAPAN MANAGED TO SPIN A COIN FOR OVER 25 SECONDS. YOU CAN BEAT THAT, RIGHT?

Attempt 1: .... seconds

Attempt 2: .... seconds

Attempt 3: .... seconds

TOO EASY? TRY THESE ...

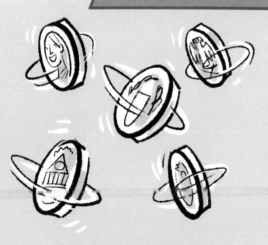

HOW MANY COINS CAN YOU SPIN AT THE SAME TIME?

CAN YOU PULL A SHEET OF PAPER OUT FROM UNDER A SPINNING COIN WITHOUT MAKING THE COIN FALL?*

*WARNING: if you manage to do this one, your friends will think you're a powerful sorcerer.

GOTCHA COVERED

Stay on this page and draw the front cover of this book without looking at it. You get one point for every part of the cover you remember.

When you're done, turn the page for the list of parts you get points for.

HOW DID YOU DO?

Total points: ....

GOTCHA COVERED
(CONTINUED)

Happy with your masterpiece? It's time to add up your score. Give yourself a point for each one of these that you remembered to include ...

- A shiny trophy

- A white cat

- A waggy-tailed dog

- A girl sticking her tongue out

- A girl with a cookie on her forehead

- A red balloon

- A boy dressed as an Egyptian pharaoh

- A girl wearing a backwards cap

- A boy throwing a bottle in the air

- A girl with a shoe on her head

Write your score on the previous page.

WEIGH TO GO

Take a set of scales and an empty container. Your mission is to fill the container with exactly 2 kilograms of stuff. You get just three attempts, so use them wisely.

Attempt 1: .... kg

Attempt 2: .... kg

Attempt 3: .... kg

QUESTION TIME

What weighs more? A 10 kg bag of cement, or a 10 kg bag of feathers? (The answer is at the bottom of the next page.)

HOW MUCH DOES STUFF WEIGH?

This handy reference guide might help you.

An adult elephant	6,000 kg
A car	1,300 kg
20 cats standing on top of each other	100 kg
A microwave	18 kg
A bowling ball	7 kg
A very big bottle of ketchup	1 kg
This book	300 g
A dung beetle	22 g
A grain of sand	0.0044 g

NO-THUMBS CHALLENGE

Eating cereal is pretty easy, right? Well let's see how you handle it ... **WITH NO THUMBS.** Get some sticky tape and ask someone to help you loosely tape your thumbs to the palms of your hands. Being able to hold stuff will soon become a thing of the past!

HOW QUICKLY CAN YOU ...

Eat a bowl of cereal? .... seconds

Open and pour a bottle of water? .... seconds

Put your coat on and fasten it up to the top? .... seconds

Hold a pen and copy out everything that's written on this page? (Use the space on the next page.) .... seconds

Question Time answer: A 10 kg bag of cement and a 10 kg bag of feathers both weigh the same, of course!

MOVE IT

How many jelly beans can you move from one bowl to another in two minutes, **without using your hands?**

Attempt 1: .... jelly beans

Attempt 2: .... jelly beans

Attempt 3: .... jelly beans

WITH A FRIEND

They have a bowl of 20 jelly beans. You have a bowl of 20 jelly beans. They have to try to get their beans into your bowl. You have to try to get your beans into their bowl. The person with the fewest beans in their bowl after two minutes wins, and you can't use your hands. **GO!**

No jelly beans at home?

UNACCEPTABLE.

Only joking — you could use any of these instead ...

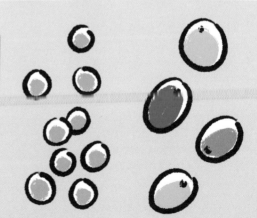

CORNFLAKES   POPCORN   PEAS   GRAPES

WATCH YOUR STEP

This challenge is all about getting from one place to another, while taking as few steps as possible. Decide on your start point, pick your finish point, and then go for it!

Attempt 1: .... steps

Attempt 2: .... steps

Attempt 3: .... steps

STEP DUEL

Take on a friend and see who can get to your finishing point in the fewest steps.

SNEAKY HINTS

ROLL ON YOUR SIDE

CRAWL

LEAP

STRETCH EACH STEP REEEEEEEEEEEALLY FAR

HAVE YOU SWALLOWED A DICTIONARY?

People seem smarter when they use big words, don't they? Words like discombobulated*, collywobbles** and Llanfairpwllgwyngyllgogerychwyrndrobwllllantysiliogogogoch*** But why use those words when you can just make up your own?

> Your challenge is to make up seven completely new words. But don't stop at just making them up — give them each a meaning, too. Write them all down here.

....

....

.... ☐

....

....

....

.... ☐

*Confused
**Tummy ache
***A village in Wales

....

....

.... ☐

....

....

.... ☐

....

....

.... ☐

....

....

.... ☐

....

....

.... ☐

For the rest of today, try to use all of your words correctly without anyone noticing that they're not real. Tick each word off as you use it.

IF YOU NEED EXTRA ROOM FOR YOUR MOST FLAMTASNIC**** WORDS, THERE'S MORE SPACE AT THE BACK OF THE BOOK.

****Not a real word.

TURN IT DOWN

For this challenge, you need to play your very favourite songs. No ordinary songs will do. We're talking **100% party bangers**.

HERE'S HOW IT WORKS

Step 1: Play one of your songs, and start singing along. Give it your all. Go you! You sound awesome!

Step 2: When about 10 seconds of your song have played, turn the volume right down so that you can't hear it any more — but keep singing.

Step 3: After another 10 seconds, turn the volume back up. Are you still singing along to the right part of the song? You are? Then give yourself a point.

Write down the names of your songs on the opposite page, and keep track of your score.

TOO EASY? TRY TURNING THE VOLUME DOWN FOR 20 SECONDS, OR EVEN 30!

Total score: ....

PRACTISE YOUR AUTOGRAPH HERE FOR WHEN YOU HIT THE BIG-TIME.

MELT AWAY

How quickly can you melt an ice cube?

THE RULES

You can't use any artificial heat sources (so no ovens, hobs, grills, microwaves, matches, fires, hair dryers or anything else sneaky like that).

You can only stop your timer when all the ice has gone and you're left with nothing but a sad, little puddle.

Attempt 1: .... seconds

Attempt 2: .... seconds

Attempt 3: .... seconds

MELTING TIPS

Lick it

Hold it tightly in your hands

Sit on it

Leave it out in the sun on a hot day

....

....

....

ADD IN YOUR OWN BEST CUBE-MELTING TACTICS

WITH A FRIEND

Take an ice cube each and have a melting race! The first person with no ice left should be crowned the ice king or queen, and move into their own massive ice palace.

I SAY POTATO

Do you say 'potato' or 'poo-tah-tyoe'?
It's a trick question. Everyone says
it the second way, obviously.

How many times in an hour can you slip the word
'potato' into conversations without anyone noticing?
It's time to find out! And remember, if anyone notices,
it's **GAME OVER** and you have to start again.

IMPORTANT SPOILY SPORT RULE

Don't do this one on
a school day. Teachers
hate potatoes and will have
you sent to potato prison
for the rest of your life.

Attempt 1: .... potatoes

Attempt 2: .... potatoes

Attempt 3: .... potatoes

GIVE THIS POTATO A FRIENDLY FACE AND A NICE NAME.

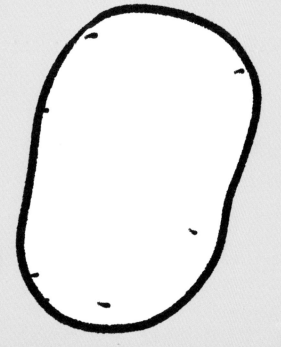

HELLO! MY NAME IS

....

SUPER BOWL

On one side of the room: you, clutching a sweet. On the other side: an empty bowl. This can only lead to one thing: you, chucking the sweet and trying to get it into the bowl.

You get 10 throws per attempt. How many make it in?

Attempt 1: .... sweets

Attempt 2: .... sweets

Attempt 3: .... sweets

MAKE IT HARDER

MOVE THE BOWL FURTHER AWAY

USE A SMALLER BOWL

THROW BLINDFOLDED

THROW WHILE LYING ON YOUR BACK

Now try playing against a friend. Fill in your scores on the opposite page to find out which of you is officially the Super Bowl Champion.

Game 1		
Game 2		
Game 3		
Game 4		
Game 5		
Game 6		
Game 7		
Game 8		
Game 9		
Game 10		
FINAL SCORE		

DRAW THE SUPER BOWL CHAMPION CELEBRATING WITH A BOWL ON THEIR HEAD HERE.

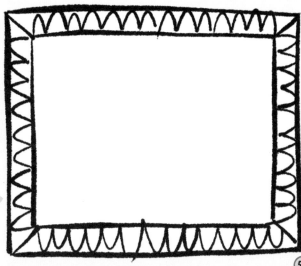

DRIBBLE TROUBLE

This isn't about yucky spit dribbling down your chin. It's about dribbling with a ball! You can do a basketball dribble (by bouncing it) or a football dribble (by kicking it), but either way, it's about showing your skills as a true **dribble master**.

Step 1: Set up your dribble course. All you have to do is put a few obstacles in a line so that you can dribble around them. Anything from toys to empty plant pots will work.

Step 2: Start your timer.

Step 3: Get dribbling! The fastest dribble is the best dribble.

Attempt 1: .... seconds

Attempt 2: .... seconds

Attempt 3: .... seconds

MAKE IT HARDER

MOVE YOUR OBSTACLES CLOSER TOGETHER

ADD A FIVE-SECOND PENALTY IF THE BALL TOUCHES AN OBSTACLE

USE A BALLOON INSTEAD OF A BALL

DRIBBLE WITH YOUR MOUTH FULL OF WATER

CAN YOU PEEL IT?

Can you peel an orange in one piece?

Here's how it's done ...

1.

2.

3.

All done? How many pieces did you

manage to unpeel it in?* ....

*If your answer is 'one', you may now devour your juicy orange with a huge sense of personal pride.

COLOUR CALAMITY

Colour in these pictures while blind-folded, then ask someone else to mark them all out of 10 to find out which one is your personal best. Don't let the other person know that you couldn't see what you were colouring, and act like you're really proud of what you've done.

AQUA
ASSAULT COURSE

This is a great game for the summertime. (Don't play it indoors, or you'll end up with a soggy floor.)

YOU'LL NEED

- Two buckets or jugs (one with water in it, and the other one empty)

- A course to run around (use toys, backpacks and anything else you can get your hands on as obstacles)

The aim is to scoop water out of the first bucket in your hands, run around the course without spilling any, and drop it off in the empty bucket. Keep going until the first bucket is empty and the second bucket is full.

If you **play against a friend** (you'll need two buckets each for that), turn it into an **AQUATIC MEGA RACE** and write the winner's name here:

....

MAKE IT HARDER

If you have a third person around, they can be your referee. The referee's job is to punish anyone spilling their water by making them stand still like a statue for **three whole seconds**. Why are referees always so mean?

STAND UP, SIT DOWN

Standing up is easy-peasy, right? Well, how about doing it **over and over again**? While only using one leg? That's right: STANDING UP JUST GOT SERIOUS.

HOW IT'S DONE

Sit on the edge of something, like a chair or your bed. One foot should always be on the ground, and the other foot should always be in the air. You're not allowed to use your hands to help you, and you're not allowed to hold onto anything.

Now ... how many times can you stand up and sit down in a minute? **GO GO GO!**

Attempt 1: .... times

Attempt 2: .... times

Attempt 3: .... times

NOW TRY IT ...

WHILE BALANCING THIS BOOK ON YOUR HEAD

WHILE SAYING THE ALPHABET BACKWARDS

WHILE THROWING AND CATCHING A BALL

WHILE GARGLING WATER

SUCK IT UP

You must now harness **THE POWER OF SUCTION**.
You need a straw, two bowls and some popcorn.
In **one minute**, how many popcorn pieces
can you move from one bowl to the other?

THE RULES

- You can only move the popcorn by sucking through the straw.

- If you use your hands, you're disqualified!

Attempt 1: .... pieces

Attempt 2: .... pieces

Attempt 3: .... pieces

WITH A FRIEND

Have a suck race! You both get two
bowls, you both get some popcorn,
and you both get one minute.

NOW TRY SUCKING ...

COTTON WOOL BALLS

PEAS

SWEETS

ANY OF THESE, BUT
WITH THREE STRAWS
TAPED TOGETHER
END-TO-END

TWO-PLAYER CHALLENGES

It's time to pit your wits against a friend, relative or sworn enemy.

DON'T MAKE ME LAUGH

The best thing about friends is that they know what makes you laugh. Sadly, in this challenge, that's also the worst thing about them.

HERE'S WHAT YOU DO:

- Two of you sit face-to-face, outdoors.

- One of you fills your mouth with water.

- Start your timer.

- You each have just one job: to make your opponent laugh.

Play best-of-three. The winner of each round is the person who manages to keep the water in their mouth the longest. And remember ... **no swallowing!**

USE YOUR DRAWING SKILLS TO MAKE THIS GUY LAUGH, TOO.

Round 1 winner: ....

Round 2 winner: ....

Round 3 winner: ....

The champion is: ....

HEAD TENNIS

To play **HEAD TENNIS** you'll need:

- One balloon

- Two people with heads

Your mission is to keep the balloon in the air, using only your heads. Each time one of you heads the balloon, count it up. Then write your totals below and show them to your grandchildren in 60 years' time so that they can see how awesome you used to be.

Attempt 1: .... headers

Attempt 2: .... headers

Attempt 3: .... headers

WHEN THE BALLOON TOUCHES THE GROUND, IT'S OVER. DON'T CRY THOUGH. NO ONE WANTS TO SEE THAT.

EXTREME HEAD TENNIS

Now play with two balloons at once!

COLOUR QUESTS

It's time for you and a friend to face-off in an almighty battle. Below is a list of colour-based quests. Each one is a race. At the end, there can only be one true champion. May fate be on your side!

Find something **blue** and bring it back ... GO!

Winner: ....

IF YOU HAVE A THIRD PERSON. THEY CAN READ OUT THE QUESTS AND IT'LL MAKE THIS GAME EVEN BETTER.

Find something **yellow** and bring it back ... GO!

Winner: ....

Find something **green** and bring it back ... GO!

Winner: ....

Find something **orange** and bring it back ... GO!

Winner: ....

Find something **red** and bring it back ... GO!

Winner: ....

Find something **black** and bring it back ... GO!

Winner: ....

Find something **purple** and bring it back ... GO!

Winner: ....

Find something **white** and bring it back ... GO!

Winner: ....

Find something **stripy** and bring it back ... GO!

Winner: ....

Find something **spotty** and bring it back ... GO!

Winner: ....

THE COLOUR QUEST CHAMPION IS ....

WHISTLE ME THIS

It's time to put your musical knowledge to the test.
Take it in turns to whistle your favourite songs.
Each time one of you works out what the other
person is whistling, you get a point.

Play best-of-five, and write who wins each round below.

WRITE YOUR NAMES HERE

Round 1		
Round 2		
Round 3		
Round 4		
Round 5		
FINAL SCORE		

TOO EASY? TRY ...

EATING A DRY CRACKER BEFORE WHISTLING

GIVING AN EXTRA POINT TO THE PERSON WHO CAN WHISTLE THE HIGHEST NOTE

WRITING LOADS OF SONG TITLES ON PIECES OF CARD, THEN PICKING ONE OUT AT RANDOM WHEN IT'S YOUR TURN

IT'S A TIE!

Who can tie a tie the fastest — you or your friend?

Make these two ties look just like your own ties, so that you remember them always:

Now, start your timer and ... **GO!**

.... **TIED THEIR TIE IN RECORD TIME (AND DON'T THEY LOOK SMART!)**

NOW TRY THESE EXTRA-TOUGH TIE RACES

TIE YOUR TIES WHILE WEARING GLOVES

TIE YOUR TIES AROUND THE TOPS OF YOUR HEADS ... AND BACKWARDS

TIE EACH OTHER'S TIES ... AT THE SAME TIME

EXTREME
ROCK PAPER SCISSORS

You've heard of Rock Paper Scissors, right? Well, this is how the pros play it. Instead of using just your hands, you use YOUR ENTIRE BODY.

HERE'S HOW IT WORKS:

ROCK
CURL UP INTO A ROCK

PAPER
LIE FLAT LIKE A SHEET OF PAPER

SCISSORS
MAKE YOURSELF SHARP!

On the count of three, you and a friend choose which shape you're going to morph into, and then unleash your full rocky papery scissory fury.

THE RULES

- Rock beats scissors (because rock blunts scissors)

- Scissors beat paper (because scissors cut paper)

- Paper beats rock (because paper gets all up in rock's face)

Basically, these guys don't get along, which is why you can never trust a rock, a piece of paper and a pair of scissors to be left alone together. Seriously. There'd be carnage.

Play best-of-five, and write your scores below ...

WRITE YOUR NAMES HERE

Game 1		
Game 2		
Game 3		
Game 4		
Game 5		
FINAL SCORE		

SURVIVAL OF THE

SMALLEST

You and a friend have two minutes to scurry off and bring back the smallest thing you can. On your marks, get set, **GO!**

SOME EXAMPLES OF SMALL THINGS

A seed
Some sand
A piece of dirt
Dust
A coffee granule
One pea
Half a bean

IMPORTANT NOTICE

THINGS THAT ARE TOO SMALL FOR ANYONE TO SEE DON'T COUNT.

.... brought back the smallest thing.

BLOW FOR IT

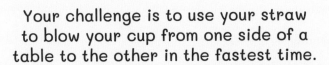

For this one, you'll need:

- A straw for each player
- A paper cup for each player
- A table top
- Lots of puff!

Your challenge is to use your straw to blow your cup from one side of a table to the other in the fastest time.

TAKE A BIG, DEEP, BREATH ... NOW BLOW!

.... is the best blower, and has earned the respect of blowers everywhere.

NO PAPER CUPS? YOU COULD USE THESE INSTEAD ...

BALLOONS

SCRUNCHED UP SHEETS OF PAPER

TOY CARS

PING PONG BALLS

MEMORY MASTERS

Try playing these memory games with a friend. At the end, add up all the scores, and then have the winner's name officially changed to **THE GREAT MEMORINO.**

Player One's name is: ....

Player Two's name is: ....

GAME 1

You both get one minute to look carefully around a room and try to remember everything that is in it. Player One then waits somewhere else, while Player Two puts five things into the room that weren't there before. Player Two then comes back into the room and has to spot the five new things. Then you swap around and play again.

Player One spotted .... things.

Player Two spotted .... things.

GAME 2

This time, Player One **removes** five things from the room, and Player Two has to come in and say what they were. Then you swap around again.

Player One noticed .... missing things.

Player Two noticed .... missing things.

GAME 3

This one's like a life-sized Spot the Difference puzzle. While Player Two is outside the room, Player One moves five things around to different places, and then Player Two has to work out what has moved. Then it's Player Two's turn to move things.

Player One noticed .... things that had moved.

Player Two noticed .... things that had moved.

USE THOSE MEMORY SKILLS TO REMEMBER TO PUT EVERYTHING BACK WHERE IT CAME FROM WHEN YOU'RE DONE!

FINAL SCORES

Player One: ....

Player Two: ....

.... is now known only as **THE GREAT MEMORINO**.

SAY ANYTHING

Only the quickest thinkers triumph in
THE SAY ANYTHING CHALLENGE.

With a friend, take it in turns to say completely random words. You can use any words you like, but you can't break these vitally important rules:

- You can only use real words.

- You can't repeat words that have already been said.

- You're not allowed to hesitate. This is a game of speed.

- You can't say 'urgh' or 'uhm' or make any other thinky noises.

The first person to break any of these rules is a
BLABBERMOUTH!

AND THE WINNER IS ....

What were the funniest words you used in your game? Make a note of them here. To make it even trickier, you're not allowed to use these the next time you play.

....

....

....

....

....

THUMB WARRIORS

One, two, three, four, it's time to declare a THUMB WAR.

CONTENDER 1

CONTENDER 2

DRAW YOURSELVES, PLEASE. THANKS.

NAME: ....

SPECIAL SKILL: ....

NAME: ....

SPECIAL SKILL: ....

LET BATTLE COMMENCE!

.... is the greatest thumb warrior.

NOW TRY THUMB WARRING ...

WHILE READING ALOUD FROM A RANDOM PAGE OF THIS BOOK

WHILE WHISTLING YOUR FAVOURITE TUNE

WITH YOUR EYES CLOSED

LIAR, LIAR

With a friend, take it in turns to say something about yourselves. Sometimes you'll tell the truth, and sometimes you'll tell a **GIGANTIC FIB**. The other person has to say if it's true or false — and each correct guess gets a point.

IT'S TIME TO TELL SOME MASSIVE WHOPPERS!

Use this handy chart to keep score. Write your names at the top and give each player a point when they guess correctly.

Your names		
Round 1		
Round 2		
Round 3		
Round 4		
Round 5		
Round 6		
Round 7		
Round 8		
Round 9		
FINAL SCORE		

Keep a record of your funniest fibs here. For especially good liars, there's also extra space at the back of the book.

....
....
....
....
....
....
....
....
....
....
....
....
....
....
....
....
....
....
....
....

WARNING

ONLY TELL LIES WHEN PLAYING THIS GAME. LYING AT ANY OTHER TIME WILL RESULT IN YOUR PANTS CATCHING FIRE.

MY DAD INVENTED THE TOOTHBRUSH.

I WAS BORN IN A CAVE.

I'M ALLERGIC TO TRUMPETS.

I CAN SPEAK TWENTY-SEVEN LANGUAGES.

HIDEY HOLES

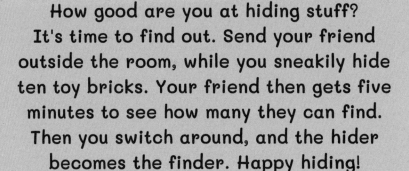

How good are you at hiding stuff?
It's time to find out. Send your friend
outside the room, while you sneakily hide
ten toy bricks. Your friend then gets five
minutes to see how many they can find.
Then you switch around, and the hider
becomes the finder. Happy hiding!

.... found .... bricks.

.... found .... bricks.

.... **is the champion!**

NOW TRY HIDING ...

YOUR SOCKS   YOURSELF   A GROWN-UP

LEAF ME ALONE

You and a friend have five minutes
to find and bring back the biggest leaf. GO!

.... found the most **monstrous** leaf.

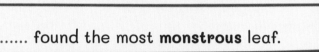

WARNING

ONLY USE LEAVES YOU FIND ON
THE GROUND. DON'T GO PULLING
LEAVES FROM HOUSE PLANTS,
OR YOU MIGHT BECOME VERY
UNPOPULAR AT HOME.

NOW FIND AND
BRING BACK ...

**THE SMALLEST
PEBBLE**

**THE SHORTEST
PENCIL**

**THE BOUNCIEST
BALL**

**THE BIGGEST
BOOK**

FINGER GOALS

Who is the **ULTIMATE FINGER GOALS CHAMPION?**
Here's how to settle the issue once and for all.

HOW TO PLAY

One of you makes a goal with your fingers, like this:

The other one sits opposite and holds a ping pong ball*
between their thumbs, like this:

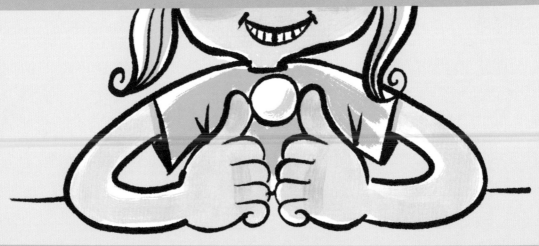

*If you don't have a ping pong ball, you could play this with a penny, sweet,
pasta shape or button. If you can shoot it from your thumbs, you can use it.

When you're both ready, the shooter launches the ball from their thumbs and tries to score. Any time you score, you must shout **'GOOOOOAAAAAALLLLLL!!!!!!!!!!'** and run around the room in celebration. That's how people will know you're serious.

PLAY BEST-OF-FIVE, TAKING IT IN TURNS TO SHOOT

.... **SCORED** .... **GOALS.**

.... **SCORED** .... **GOALS.**

MAKE IT HARDER

SHOOT FROM DOUBLE THE DISTANCE

GIVE EACH PLAYER JUST TWO SECONDS TO TAKE THEIR SHOT

PUT SOME TOYS BETWEEN YOU AS OBSTACLES

MAKE THE
TALLEST HAT

Hats are great! They're like clothes for your hair. The bigger your hat, the better you feel, and the more awesome you look. That's why you're now going to make the **biggest hat** of your tiny life.

With a friend, take 30 minutes, and get hat-making. At the end, the person with the tallest hat wins.

THE RULES

- You can't use anything that is already a hat.

- You have to be able to wear your new hat on your head for at least 30 seconds without it falling off.

- It must look like an actual hat.

DRAW THE WINNING HAT HERE

MAKE THE
SMALLEST HAT

Now you know how **brilliant** tall hats are, but did you know that small hats are **ace** too? The best thing about a small hat is that you can wear it underneath a bigger hat (as a general rule, the more hats you wear, the more legendary you are).

With a friend, take 30 minutes, and see who can make the tiniest hat. Smallest wins!

THE RULES

• You can't just cut bits off your big hat.

• You have to be able to wear it on your head (you might want to wear it out to a nice restaurant, for example).

• It must look like an actual hat (so no just putting an ant on your head and saying it's a hat, sorry).

DRAW THE WINNING HAT HERE

READ MY LIPS

For this one, you need a friend and a pair of headphones. One of you wears the headphones and listens to your favourite tunes. The other one says something out loud. It could be a phrase, or a celebrity's name, or a TV show. The person wearing the headphones has to try to figure out what the other person is saying, just by reading their lips.

KEEP A NOTE OF YOUR SCORES HERE. EACH TIME SOMEONE GETS ONE RIGHT, PUT A TICK UNDER THEIR NAME.

PLAYER 1: ....

PLAYER 2: ....

THE WINNER IS: ....

Stuck for things to say? Try using the spare pages at the back of this book to write down some ideas before you get started.

You could also write loads of phrases on cards, mix them up, and pull out a new card each time it's your turn.

AGAINST THE WALL

You and a friend take five toy bricks* each.
Your bricks should all be one colour, and
your friend's bricks should all be another
colour. Take it in turns to throw your bricks
against an outside wall. Once you've both
thrown all your bricks, the winner is the
person who has a brick closest to the wall.

RULES ARE (NOT) FOR FOOLS

• Your brick has to be thrown. You can't slide it,
or roll it, or do anything else that isn't a throw.

• You both have to stand the same distance from the wall.

AND THE WINNER IS ...
(DRUMROLL SOUND PLEASE)

....

MAKE IT HARDER

STAND AS FAR FROM THE
WALL AS POSSIBLE AND TRY
SOME LONG THROWS

STAND WITH YOUR BACKS TO
THE WALL, AND CHUCK YOUR
BRICKS BACKWARDS OVER YOUR
SHOULDERS WITHOUT LOOKING

*If you don't have any bricks, you could use sweets or pennies.